e last
irrent
letter
>wer

JOHN BETJEMAN

Hugo Williams was born in 1942 and grew up in Sussex. He worked on the *London Magazine* from 1961 to 1970, since when he has earned his living as a journalist and travel writer. *Billy's Rain* won the T. S. Eliot Prize in 1999. His *Collected Poems* was published by Faber in 2002 and his last collection, *Dear Room*, was published in 2006. His new collection, *West End Final*, will be published in Summer 2009. Hugo Williams lives in London.

JOHN BETJEMAN

Poems selected by HUGO WILLIAMS

faber and faber

A selection of work by one of the great poets of the twentieth century, with a specially commissioned cover by Joe McLaren, to mark Faber's eightieth anniversary

First published in 2006 by
Faber and Faber Ltd
Bloomsbury House
74–77 Great Russell Street
London WC1B 3DA
This special 80th Anniversary edition first published in 2009

Printed in England by
CPI Mackays, Chatham, ME5 8TD

The right of John Betjeman to be identified as author of this work has been asserted in accordance with Section 77 of the Copyright, Designs and Patents Act 1988

The right of Hugo Williams to be identified as editor of this work has been asserted in accordance with Section 77 of the Copyright, Designs and Patents Act 1988

A CIP record for this book
is available from the British Library

ISBN 978–0–571–24702–8

10 9 8 7 6 5 4 3 2 1

Contents

Introduction

John Betjeman makes most modern poets look either desperately amateurish or desperately professional. A combination of happy childhood, miserable schooldays and Oxford in the 1920s gave him a pretty balanced view of who he was and what he could do and he never lost sight of this. If you haven't read him before you're taken aback by how good he is. A festive, holiday atmosphere hangs over his work: no wonder nobody mentioned him at school. Like any writer you discover for yourself, he becomes a covert favourite, one whose name you are inclined to drop into conversations, sounding out the company. At home, you keep him on that special shelf near your chair. And this may be the secret of his success – reading him is an act of mild anarchy. It's worth remembering that Philip Larkin kept Betjeman on his own special shelf, alongside Hardy, Lawrence and Christina Rossetti.

Reading the *Collected Poems* from beginning to end, an impossibility with most modern poets, you can't help admiring how he stuck to his original vision throughout a long writing life. No nonsense about development for him. He started good and he stayed good. Socially, he was seduced as an undergraduate out of the middle class and into the upper class, where people were notionally freer, gayer and more fun, but artistically he remained true to his roots and so we have the marvellous satirical poems of lost suburban proprieties and aspirations. His was the great age of nostalgia when everything in England was sliding under the scum of cash. Nowadays everything passes away so quickly on the tide that there is no time for Betjeman's brand of lyricism even to recognise it, let alone pin it down so fervently. His example remains open.

I don't want to make a great case for Betjeman being a lost major figure: Larkin has done that already: 'Reading Mr Betjeman's latest book of poems [*A Few Late Chrysanthemums*], I am left with the feeling that in some astonishing unacknowledged way he has crept up with the leaders.' But who's to say where he might have stood (and may yet stand) in the canon if modernism hadn't been there to make a joke out of him and his work – and thus he of himself in his defence. After spending time with John Betjeman, most other modern poets seem curiously introverted, depending too much on self-generated production standards. Their work seems to lose sight of who they are and sets out instead on a great journey to the land of literature. Reading the most respected modern poetry, you are immediately confronted by problems of comprehension which it takes another book to resolve. Betjeman by comparison competes by existing rules. He lays out his wares for us to judge by our own standards, not his. Instead of a manifesto we get the whole man. He is constantly experimenting with words, but never to the extent of losing his reader's complicity. We don't need him on the syllabuses because he has thoughtlessly taken out all the difficulty himself during the writing of the poem. We see him roaring with laughter on his book covers and feel we know who he is laughing at.

Not that he didn't have to fight his own way out of modernism. If T. S. Eliot secretly learnt more from Arthur Symons than he did from Dante, Betjeman went the other way: 'Frightfully good, old Newbolt,' etc, when in fact he was reading Eliot and Auden like everyone else. An early *vox populi* pub poem of Betjeman's, 'Clash Went the Billiard Balls', is straight from Part II of *The Waste Land.* Eliot: 'Goonight Bill. Goonight Lou. Goonight May.' Betjeman: 'Goodnight, Alf! Goodnight, Bert! Goodnight, Mrs Gilligan!' His 'Monody on the Death of Aldersgate Street Station' attempts to make readable the theme of architecture mirroring moral decline in Part III of Eliot's *The Rock.* Eliot: 'We built in vain unless the Lord built with us. / Can you keep the City that the Lord keeps not with you??' Betjeman: 'For us of the steam and the gaslight, the lost generation,/ The new white cliffs of the City are built in vain.' In 'Senex' – 'Oh would I could subdue the flesh' – written when he was thirty-four, he mimics, for a laugh, the premature senescences of J. Alfred Prufrock. (He complained in old age that he wished he'd had more sex.) In 'Felixstowe, or The Last of Her Order' he manages to evoke both 'Prufrock' and 'Dover Beach', probably deliberately: 'With one consuming roar along the shingle/ The long wave claws and rakes the pebbles down / To where its backwash and the next wave mingle.' He eventually got round to a little gentle mockery: 'Rime Intrinsica, Fontmell Magna, Sturminster Newton and Melbury

Bubb,/ Whist upon whist upon whist upon whist drive, in Institute, Legion and Social Club.' His satire is rarely spiteful, although an exception might be made for 'May-Day Song for North Oxford', in which he makes an obscure (to me) joke at the expense of the Oxford don who sabotaged his degree: 'Oh! earnest ethical search/ For the wide high table λογοδ of St C. S. Lewis's Church', taking care to point out that it should be sung to the 'Annie Laurie Tune'. I wonder was it a turning point, the moment when he stopped admiring the problematical stuff which stood beyond the average reader's unassisted critical appraisal and turned his head towards the harder, unprotected world of ordinary excellence.

He was perhaps nudged in this direction by the taste he developed at Oxford for titled folk and posh totty, a section of the community not known for their tolerance of experimental art. It would have been important for him not to look like an inky little swot in this company. He set his sights at their very high boredom levels and dug in for the duration. It is this early class affiliation which set him apart from his modernist and left-wing contemporaries and steered him towards the subject matter of some of his most famous poems – satirical stuff and music hall turns about the funny middle classes and their suburban living habits. His early worldliness enabled him to gauge the specific gravity of such themes, their literary density, how much weight they would take, at what length; above all, what key they were in.

The frisson of upward mobility is memorably caught in 'A Subaltern's Love-Song' about the famous Miss Joan Hunter Dunn. The poem moves with the pace and timing of a good movie – from the tennis court to the verandah for lime juice and gin, back to his room to change, thence to her own room at the same moment for the essential blazer and shorts to be seen scattered on the floor, to picking her up later for the dance, then the short car ride in the Hillman, 'by roads not adopted', to the golf club car park, where they sit, presumably necking, 'till twenty to one/ And now I'm engaged to Miss Joan Hunter Dunn.' The whole thing is a wonderful swooping dolley-shot of a poem, not unlike the spectacular opening crane-shot in *Touch of Evil*. It is customary to praise writers of all kinds, especially poets, for being 'cinematic', but it is more likely that good films mimic the traditional techniques of good poetry: silent film scripts were often written as poems. Betjeman, a sometime film critic for the *Evening Standard*, was less than modern in his subject matter and verse forms, but his techniques of montage, cutting, fades and close-ups make him modern in spite of himself. This is most noticeable in early poems like 'The Flight from Bootle' (rhymes with 'footle') about a Regent Palace Hotel pick-up: 'Time for me to go and scrounge' – rhyming naturally with 'lounge'. The second verse is a premature flashback, which we accept easily enough, such is his directorial skill.

You only have to look at a poem like 'Myfanwy' – one of his most emotionally naked – to feel the camera leading you effortlessly back and forth across the generations, as the grown Myfanwy bicycles 'out of the shopping and into the dark,/ Back down the avenue, back to the pottingshed,/ Back to the house on the fringe of the park' where the adolescent Betjeman first saw and fell in love with her, playing sardines at a party. Before we reach the Fuller's angel-cake we see the motherly Myfanwy one more time, reading to her own children: 'Golden the light on the book on her knee,/ Finger-marked pages of Rackham's Hans Andersen,/ Time for the children to come down to tea.' The poem collapses the generations with such assurance – were they her own childish finger-marks on the pages? – that they blend on the page just as they do in life. The montage of images, immediately moving, only gradually reveals its meaning as the generations extricate themselves at subsequent readings. The confusion echoes his own slight embarrassment. Is she a child or a mother? Is she a girl he once knew and lost touch with and longs for still, remembering her childhood beauty? Or just the wife of a friend? Larkin talks somewhere about the need to give the reader something to be going along with, while reserving something more to repay closer scrutiny. Betjeman manages this with cinematic blurrings of time and space.

There is a recurring theme of childhood sexuality in Betjeman, which puts him ahead of his time. Who else would dare combine, as in 'Indoor Games near Newbury', a celebration of a middle-class children's party with vaguely underage lust, nicely rhyming ' "Choose your partners for a fox-trot! Dance until it's *tea* o'clock!" ' with 'hard against your party frock'? It may be slightly arch, but thank God someone wasn't too timid to record what was certainly my own experience of the days before 'teen', when adolescents counted as children and parties with Vimto and marshmallows shaded off into dancing in the dark.

To have conjured, in a poem like 'Parliament Hill Fields', a whole childhood from the fugitive material of the recent past and made it hearable, tasteable and smellable to the modern reader is Betjeman's special gift. 'Middlesex', another key poem, reveals his homesickness for the secure social position and innocent aspirations of the class he grew out of. In this he is the Tony Harrison of his generation.

> Well cut Windsmoor flapping lightly,
>   Jacqmar scarf of mauve and green
> Hiding hair which, Friday nightly,
>   Delicately drowns in Drene;
> Fair Elaine the bobby-soxer,
> Fresh-complexioned with Innoxa,
> Gains the garden – father's hobby –
> Hangs her Windsmoor in the lobby,
> Settles down to sandwich supper and the television
>   screen.

It is not so easy to look at your own time with such a cool eye and single out those things which distinguish it; only in retrospect do they seem obvious. One has only to think of one's own period to have a sensation of drowning in detail. Betjeman kept his nerve. Or did he just keep a notebook? Many of the poems seem vehicles for strong lines and jokes of the kind that can't be made up. 'Devilled chicken. Devilled whitebait. Devil if I understand,' complains the old poet in the Café Royal. (He should see it today.) Will Wembley ever be free of 'trembley' since he shackled them? Was it 'He who trained a hundred winners/ Paid the Final Entrance fee' that set him off on 'Upper Lambourne', his racing tribute? And was it Cheltenham's funny word for a mortarboard that started him on

> 'Shall I forget the warm marquee
>   And the General's wife so soon,
> When my son's colleger acted as tray
>   For an ice and a maccaroon?'

He writes on the hoof, out of doors, in trains, and the great poems seem to get written by happy chance, out of an impulse to speak his mind. A kind of drunkenness of sentiment comes over him when he writes about something that moves him. 'Youth and Age on Beaulieu River' concludes,

> Clemency, the General's daughter,
>   Will return upon the flood.
> But the older woman only
> Knows the ebb-tide leaves her lonely
>   With the shining fields of mud.

It is so good it almost disappears, leaving us with the horrifying transcendence of a single word, 'shining'. 'Invasion Exercise on the Poultry Farm' might have been a rhymed film script about the quiet wartime menage of two home-counties lesbians whose peace is shattered by the arrival of paratroopers in the area:

> Softly croons the radiogram, loudly hoot the owls,
> Judy gives the door a slam and goes to feed the fowls.
> Marty rolls a Craven A around her ruby lips
> And runs her yellow fingers down her corduroyed hips.

'Corduroyed' looks wrong at first, but then you remember who you're talking to. The hoot isn't that of an owl, unfortunately for Marty, who, if she were straight, wouldn't be smoking Craven A. I love the way he makes a point of crediting, in a footnote, a couple of lines to a friend, as if the whole perfectly-pitched exercise were an after-dinner joke. No midnight oil on him! And yet if he ever permitted us to pause we might glimpse a more recalcitrant material from which such casual brilliance had been persuaded to unfold. I wonder from what inauspicious lump of rock he carved the unforgettable image of the couple 'In a Bath Teashop': how many hours it took, how much associated material fell to the cutting-room floor. This is the technique of a poet who routinely put our needs before his own, an unfashionable priority in the aftermath of modernism. Reading the poem again, I still can't decide if it's the beginning or end of the story; the ramifications are infinite.

Another poem which seems to have left most of itself out for our benefit, but whose longer self is still vestigially present, is 'On Seeing an Old Poet in the Café Royal'. Meeting this washed-up relic of the 1890s, I can't help wondering who he is. Oscar Wilde, Alfred Douglas and Theodore Wratislaw are all mentioned in the old poet's ramblings, so he can't be them. Most of the poets of the 90s died young, long before Betjeman could have caught sight of one of them doddering over his 'Tutti-Frutti-Sen-Sen'. It has to be someone who was still alive as late as 1933, when Wratislaw died. Richard Le Gallienne and Ernest Rhys were still around, as was Henry Newbolt, a Betjeman perennial, but my guess is it was Arthur Symons (1865–1945), whose earlier destructive breakdown had caused him to suffer delusions. It doesn't sound like Yeats.

We don't think of Betjeman being a particularly autobiographical poet, but his work is full of personal, even confessional details. 'Portrait of a Deaf Man' is to all intents a miniature self-portrait done in the third person. 'He liked old City dining rooms . . . rain-washed Cornish air . . .' Who does he think he's fooling? The reason 'He took me on long silent walks' was because he was on his own. After all the redemptive bells and such, it is a relief to hear him speaking frankly to his God: 'You ask me to believe You and/ I only see decay'. Again, the rawness of 'Pershore Station' can't quite be accounted for by that bluff subtitle, 'A Liverish Journey First Class':

I remembered her defencelessness as I made my heart a stone
Till she wove her self-protection round her and left me on my
   own.
And plunged in deep self-pity I dreamed of another wife
And lusted for freckled faces and lived a separate life.

It's hard to think of any other modern poet who has appeared in public with less on.

Even his breezy Cornish poems ambush us with tides of anxiety. It seems his strength of purpose, his famous 'whim of iron', was mostly illusory:

Gigantic slithering shelves of slate
In waiting awfulness appear
   Like journalism full of hate . . .

And I on my volcano edge
    Exposed to ridicule and hate
Still do not dare to leap the ledge . . .
                        ('Tregardock')

For every 'I made hay while the sun shone./ My work sold', there is
a counterweight:

When I'm sweating a lot
    From the strain on a last bit of lung
And lust has gone out
    Leaving only the things of the brain;
More worthless than ever
    Will seem all the songs I have sung . . .
                        ('Goodbye')

Even if a few pages later he is feeling better again:

Here where the cliffs alone prevail
    I stand exultant, neutral, free . . .
                        ('Winter Seas')

I suspect he put more time and effort into writing about the
seaside and the country than he ever did about suburbia. He gets it
right so often, of course: 'The wideness which the lark-song gives the
sky.' But effort isn't everything; the country has been done, as it were:
suburbia is what we want to hear about, if possible before the
Department of Suburban Studies gets hold of it.

I remember his daughter Candida describing her despair on
family car trips as a child: 'Oh Dad, not *another* old church!' 'The
Cockney Amorist', about a London courtship, owns up to this. It
would have been improved without the flat second verse about
church visiting: 'I'll use them now for praying in/ And not for
looking round' (no wonder she took off). The last verse is spot on,
but we risk not getting there:

I love you, oh my darling,
    And what I can't make out
Is why since you have left me
    I'm somehow still about.

You sometimes feel like complaining how many poems are spoilt by piety; after the halfway point you search increasingly for things without bells in them. You'd rather they were 'belles'. He comes across like Quasimodo in his belfry. But after all, this is John Betjeman, he can do what he likes. And anyway, you find out so much more about a poet from his less successful poems because he is seen in a moment of weakness. True thoughts show through such poems because they give the lie to the difficult places his character wanted to go once it had been everywhere else. To come upon a man's odd failure is to admire him anew as you realise how hard he worked to find his successes and what they must have meant to him.

It is standard practice to talk about Betjeman's obsession with death and religion as if that gained for him some needed seriousness, when actually such fears come far behind the dominant notes of humour, celebration and joy, which are much harder to get right. If he has a well-developed sense of his mortality it is no more than any poet needs to make poetry out of.

His taste for suburban railway stations, provincial art galleries, small-print pocket books, insects, jellyfish, Australia, Mary Wilson, impoverished Irish peers and minor public schools were affectations in solidarity with the (then) unpopular public buildings he fought so hard to save and which he identified with, having been bullied himself at school. (The Eurostar wouldn't be coming grandly into St Pancras if it weren't for Sir John.) All this he worked at; what he was born with was a natural excitability and a diamond-stylus ear for a particular English music:

Has it held, the warm June weather?
    Draining shallow sea-pools dry,
When we bicyled together
    Down the bohreens fuchsia-high.

The question combines the power of memory with the power of language to track over time and space. Has it held? Has it held? I think we can say it has.

Hugo Williams

JOHN BETJEMAN

Death in Leamington

She died in the upstairs bedroom
　　By the light of the ev'ning star
That shone through the plate glass window
　　From over Leamington Spa.

Beside her the lonely crochet
　　Lay patiently and unstirred,
But the fingers that would have work'd it
　　Were dead as the spoken word.

And Nurse came in with the tea-things
　　Breast high 'mid the stands and chairs –
But Nurse was alone with her own little soul,
　　And the things were alone with theirs.

She bolted the big round window,
　　She let the blinds unroll,
She set a match to the mantle,
　　She covered the fire with coal.

And 'Tea!' she said in a tiny voice
　　'Wake up! It's nearly *five*.'
Oh! Chintzy, chintzy cheeriness,
　　Half dead and half alive!

Do you know that the stucco is peeling?
　　Do you know that the heart will stop?
From those yellow Italianate arches
　　Do you hear the plaster drop?

Nurse looked at the silent bedstead,
　　At the gray, decaying face,
As the calm of a Leamington ev'ning
　　Drifted into the place.

She moved the table of bottles
    Away from the bed to the wall;
And tiptoeing gently over the stairs
    Turned down the gas in the hall.

The 'Varsity Students' Rag

I'm afraid the fellows in Putney rather wish they had
The social ease and manners of a 'varsity undergrad,
For tho' they're awf'lly decent and up to a lark as a rule
You want to have the 'varsity touch after a public school.

CHORUS:
We had a rag at Monico's. *We* had a rag at the Troc.,
And the one we had at the Berkeley gave the customers
quite a shock.
Then we went to the Popular, and after that – oh my!
I *wish* you'd seen the rag we had in the Grill Room at
the Cri.

I started a rag in Putney at our Frothblower's Branch down
there;
We got in a damn'd old lorry and drove to Trafalgar Square;
And we each had a couple of toy balloons and made the hell
of a din,
And I saw a bobby at Parson's Green who looked like running
us in.

CHORUS: We, etc.

But that's nothing to the rag we had at the college the other
night;
We'd gallons and gallons of cider – and I got frightfully
tight.
And then we smash'd up ev'rything, and what was the
funniest part
We smashed some rotten old pictures which were priceless
works of art.

CHORUS: We, etc.

There's something about a 'varsity man that distinguishes him
from a cad:

5

You can tell by his tie and blazer he's a 'varsity undergrad,
And you know that he's always ready and up to a bit of a lark,
With a toy balloon and a whistle and some cider after dark.

   CHORUS: We, etc.

The Wykehamist

(To Randolph Churchill, but not about him.)

Broad of Church and broad of mind,
Broad before and broad behind,
A keen ecclesiologist,
A rather dirty Wykehamist.
'Tis not for us to wonder why
He wears that curious knitted tie;
We should not cast reflections on
The very slightest kind of don.
We should not giggle as we like
At his appearance on his bike;
It's something to become a bore,
And more than that, at twenty-four.
It's something too to know your wants
And go full pelt for Norman fonts.
Just now the chestnut trees are dark
And full with shadow in the park,
And 'six o'clock!' St Mary calls
Above the mellow college walls.
The evening stretches arms to twist
And captivate her Wykehamist.
But not for him these autumn days,
He shuts them out with heavy baize;
He gives his Ovaltine a stir
And nibbles at a 'petit beurre',
And, satisfying fleshy wants,
He settles down to Norman fonts.

The Arrest of Oscar Wilde at the Cadogan Hotel

He sipped at a weak hock and seltzer
  As he gazed at the London skies
Through the Nottingham lace of the curtains
  Or was it his bees-winged eyes!

To the right and before him Pont Street
  Did tower in her new built red,
As hard as the morning gaslight
  That shone on his unmade bed,

'I want some more hock in my seltzer,
  And Robbie, please give me your hand –
Is this the end or beginning?
  How can I understand?

'So you've brought me the latest *Yellow Book*:
  And Buchan has got in it now:
Approval of what is approved of
  Is as false as a well-kept vow.

'More hock, Robbie – where is the seltzer?
  Dear boy, pull again at the bell!
They are all little better than *cretins*,
  Though this *is* the Cadogan Hotel.

'One astrakhan coat is at Willis's –
  Another one's at the Savoy:
Do fetch my morocco portmanteau,
  And bring them on later, dear boy.'

A thump, and a murmur of voices –
  ('Oh why must they make such a din?')
As the door of the bedroom swung open
  And TWO PLAIN CLOTHES POLICEMEN came in:

'Mr Woilde, we 'ave come for tew take yew
  Where felons and criminals dwell:
We must ask yew tew leave with us quoietly
  For this *is* the Cadogan Hotel.'

He rose, and he put down *The Yellow Book.*
  He staggered – and, terrible-eyed,
He brushed past the palms on the staircase
  And was helped to a hansom outside.

Slough

Come, friendly bombs, and fall on Slough
It isn't fit for humans now,
There isn't grass to graze a cow
   Swarm over, Death!

Come, bombs, and blow to smithereens
Those air-conditioned, bright canteens,
Tinned fruit, tinned meat, tinned milk, tinned beans
   Tinned minds, tinned breath.

Mess up the mess they call a town –
A house for ninety-seven down
And once a week a half-a-crown
   For twenty years,

And get that man with double chin
Who'll always cheat and always win,
Who washes his repulsive skin
   In women's tears,

And smash his desk of polished oak
And smash his hands so used to stroke
And stop his boring dirty joke
   And make him yell.

But spare the bald young clerks who add
The profits of the stinking cad;
It's not their fault that they are mad,
   They've tasted Hell.

It's not their fault they do not know
The birdsong from the radio,
It's not their fault they often go
   To Maidenhead

And talk of sports and makes of cars
In various bogus Tudor bars
And daren't look up and see the stars
    But belch instead.

In labour-saving homes, with care
Their wives frizz out peroxide hair
And dry it in synthetic air
    And paint their nails.

Come, friendly bombs, and fall on Slough
To get it ready for the plough.
The cabbages are coming now;
    The earth exhales.

Love in a Valley

Take me, Lieutenant, to that Surrey homestead!
  Red comes the winter and your rakish car,
Red among the hawthorns, redder than the hawberries
  And trails of old man's nuisance, and noisier far.
Far, far below me roll the Coulsdon woodlands,
  White down the valley curves the living rail,*
Tall, tall, above me, olive spike the pinewoods,
  Olive against blue-black, moving in the gale.

Deep down the drive go the cushioned rhododendrons,
  Deep down, sand deep, drives the heather root,
Deep the spliced timber barked around the summer-house,
  Light lies the tennis-court, plantain underfoot.
What a winter welcome to what a Surrey homestead!
  Oh! the metal lantern and white enamelled door!
Oh! the spread of orange from the gas-fire on the carpet!
  Oh! the tiny patter, sandalled footsteps on the floor!

Fling wide the curtains! – that's a Surrey sunset
  Low down the line sings the Addiscombe train,
Leaded are the windows lozenging the crimson,
  Drained dark the pines in resin-scented rain.
Portable Lieutenant! they carry you to China
  And me to lonely shopping in a brilliant arcade;
Firm hand, fond hand, switch the giddy engine!
  So for us a last time is bright light made.

* Southern Electric 25 mins.

An Impoverished Irish Peer

Within that parsonage
There is a personage
Who owns a mortgage
   On his Lordship's land,
On his fine plantations,
Well speculated,
With groves of beeches
   On either hand –
On his ten ton schooner
Upon Loch Gowna,
And the silver birches
   Along the land –
Where the little pebbles
Do sing like trebles
As the waters bubble
   Upon the strand –

On his gateway olden
Of plaster moulded
And his splendid carriage way
   To Castle Grand,
(They've been aquatinted
For a book that's printed
And even wanted
   In far England)
His fine saloons there
Would make you swoon, sir,
And each surrounded
   By a gilded band –
And 'tis there Lord Ashtown
Lord Trimlestown and
Clonmore's Lord likewise
   Are entertained.

As many flunkeys
As Finnea has donkeys
Are there at all times
    At himself's a command.
Though he doesn't pay them
They all obey him
And would sure die for him
    If he waved his hand;
Yet if His Lordship
Comes for to worship
At the Holy Table
    To take his stand,
Though humbly kneeling
There's no fair dealing
And no kind feeling
    In the parson's hand.
Preaching of Liberty
Also of Charity
In the grand high pulpit
    To see him stand,
You'ld think that personage
In that parsonage
Did own no mortgage
    On His Lordship's land.

Death of King George V

'New King arrives in his capital by air . . .' – Daily Newspaper

Spirits of well-shot woodcock, partridge, snipe
    Flutter and bear him up the Norfolk sky:
In that red house in a red mahogany book-case
    The stamp collection waits with mounts long dry.

The big blue eyes are shut which saw wrong clothing
    And favourite fields and coverts from a horse;
Old men in country houses hear clocks ticking
    Over thick carpets with a deadened force;

Old men who never cheated, never doubted,
    Communicated monthly, sit and stare
At the new suburb stretched beyond the run-way
    Where a young man lands hatless from the air.

The Flight from Bootle

Lonely in the Regent Palace,
  Sipping her 'Banana Blush',
Lilian lost sight of Alice
  In the honey-coloured rush.

Settled down at last from Bootle,
  Alice whispered, 'Just a min,
While I pop upstairs and rootle
  For another safety pin.'

Dreamy from the band pavilion
  Drops of the *Immortal Hour*
Fell around the lonely Lilian
  Like an ineffectual shower.

Half an hour she sat and waited
  In the honey-coloured lounge
Till she with herself debated,
  'Time for me to go and scrounge!'

Time enough! or not enough time!
  Lilian, you wait in vain;
Alice will not have a rough time,
  Nor be quite the same again.

A Shropshire Lad

*N.B. – This should be recited with a Midland accent.
Captain Webb, the swimmer and a relation of Mary Webb
by marriage, was born at Dawley in an industrial district in
Salop.*

The gas was on in the Institute,*
    The flare was up in the gym,
A man was running a mineral line,
    A lass was singing a hymn,
When Captain Webb the Dawley man,
    Captain Webb from Dawley,
Came swimming along the old canal
    That carried the bricks to Lawley.
        Swimming along –
        Swimming along –
        Swimming along from Severn,
And paying a call at Dawley Bank while swimming along to
    Heaven.

The sun shone low on the railway line
    And over the bricks and stacks,
And in at the upstairs windows
    Of the Dawley houses' backs,
When we saw the ghost of Captain Webb,
    Webb in a water sheeting,
Come dripping along in a bathing dress
    To the Saturday evening meeting.
        Dripping along –
        Dripping along –
        To the Congregational Hall;
Dripping and still he rose over the sill and faded away in a
    wall.

There wasn't a man in Oakengates
    That hadn't got hold of the tale,

And over the valley in Ironbridge,
　　And round by Coalbrookdale,
How Captain Webb the Dawley man,
　　Captain Webb from Dawley,
Rose rigid and dead from the old canal
　　That carries the bricks to Lawley.
　　　　Rigid and dead –
　　　　Rigid and dead –
　　　　To the Saturday congregation,
Paying a call at Dawley Bank on his way to his destination.

* 'The Institute was radiant with gas.' Ch. XIX, *Boyhood*. A novel in verse
by Rev. E. E. Bradford, D.D.

Upper Lambourne

Up the ash-tree climbs the ivy,
    Up the ivy climbs the sun,
With a twenty-thousand pattering
    Has a valley breeze begun,
Feathery ash, neglected elder,
    Shift the shade and make it run –

Shift the shade toward the nettles,
    And the nettles set it free
To streak the stained Carrara headstone
    Where, in nineteen-twenty-three,
He who trained a hundred winners
    Paid the Final Entrance Fee.

Leathery limbs of Upper Lambourne,
    Leathery skin from sun and wind,
Leathery breeches, spreading stables,
    Shining saddles left behind –
To the down the string of horses
    Moving out of sight and mind.

Feathery ash in leathery Lambourne
    Waves above the sarsen stone,
And Edwardian plantations
    So coniferously moan
As to make the swelling downland,
    Far-surrounding, seem their own.

On Seeing an Old Poet in the Café Royal

I saw him in the Café Royal.
  Very old and very grand.
Modernistic shone the lamplight
  There in London's fairyland.
    'Devilled chicken. Devilled whitebait.
    Devil if I understand.

Where is Oscar? Where is Bosie?
  Have I seen that man before?
And the old one in the corner,
  Is it really Wratislaw?'
Scent of Tutti-Frutti-Sen-Sen
  And cheroots upon the floor.

Trebetherick

We used to picnic where the thrift
  Grew deep and tufted to the edge;
We saw the yellow foam-flakes drift
  In trembling sponges on the ledge
Below us, till the wind would lift
  Them up the cliff and o'er the hedge.
Sand in the sandwiches, wasps in the tea,
Sun on our bathing-dresses heavy with the wet,
Squelch of the bladder-wrack waiting for the sea,
Fleas round the tamarisk, an early cigarette.

From where the coastguard houses stood
  One used to see, below the hill,
The lichened branches of a wood
  In summer silver-cool and still;
And there the Shade of Evil could
  Stretch out at us from Shilla Mill.
Thick with sloe and blackberry, uneven in the light,
Lonely ran the hedge, the heavy meadow was remote,
The oldest part of Cornwall was the wood as black as night,
And the pheasant and the rabbit lay torn open at the throat.

But when a storm was at its height,
  And feathery slate was black in rain,
And tamarisks were hung with light
  And golden sand was brown again,
Spring tide and blizzard would unite
  And sea came flooding up the lane.
Waves full of treasure then were roaring up the beach,
Ropes round our mackintoshes, waders warm and dry,
We waited for the wreckage to come swirling into reach,
Ralph, Vasey, Alastair, Biddy, John and I.

Then roller into roller curled
     And thundered down the rocky bay,
And we were in a water-world
     Of rain and blizzard, sea and spray,
And one against the other hurled
     We struggled round to Greenaway.
Blessèd be St Enodoc, blessèd be the wave,
Blessèd be the springy turf, we pray, pray to thee,
Ask for our children all the happy days you gave
To Ralph, Vasey, Alastair, Biddy, John and me.

Myfanwy

Kind o'er the *kinderbank* leans my Myfanwy,
  White o'er the play-pen the sheen of her dress,
Fresh from the bathroom and soft in the nursery
  Soap-scented fingers I long to caress.

Were you a prefect and head of your dormit'ry?
  Were you a hockey girl, tennis or gym?
Who was your favourite? Who had a crush on you?
  Which were the baths where they taught you to swim?

Smooth down the Avenue glitters the bicycle,
  Black-stockinged legs under navy-blue serge,
Home and Colonial, Star, International,
  Balancing bicycle leant on the verge.

Trace me your wheel-tracks, you fortunate bicycle,
  Out of the shopping and into the dark,
Back down the Avenue, back to the pottingshed,
  Back to the house on the fringe of the park.

Golden the light on the locks of Myfanwy,
  Golden the light on the book on her knee,
Finger-marked pages of Rackham's Hans Andersen,
  Time for the children to come down to tea.

Oh! Fuller's angel-cake, Robertson's marmalade,
  Liberty lampshade, come, shine on us all,
My! what a spread for the friends of Myfanwy
  Some in the alcove and some in the hall.

Then what sardines in the half-lighted passages!
  Locking of fingers in long hide-and-seek.
You will protect me, my silken Myfanwy,
  Ringleader, tom-boy, and chum to the weak.

Senex

Oh would I could subdue the flesh
    Which sadly troubles me!
And then perhaps could view the flesh
As though I never knew the flesh
    And merry misery.

To see the golden hiking girl
    With wind about her hair,
The tennis-playing, biking girl,
The wholly-to-my-liking girl,
    To see and not to care.

At sundown on my tricycle
    I tour the Borough's edge,
And icy as an icicle
See bicycle by bicycle
    Stacked waiting in the hedge.

Get down from me! I thunder there,
    You spaniels! Shut your jaws!
Your teeth are stuffed with underwear,
Suspenders torn asunder there
    And buttocks in your paws!

Oh whip the dogs away my Lord,
    They make me ill with lust.
Bend bare knees down to pray, my Lord,
Teach sulky lips to say, my Lord,
    That flaxen hair is dust.

On a Portrait of a Deaf Man

The kind old face, the egg-shaped head,
    The tie, discreetly loud,
The loosely fitting shooting clothes,
    A closely fitting shroud.

He liked old City dining-rooms,
    Potatoes in their skin,
But now his mouth is wide to let
    The London clay come in.

He took me on long silent walks
    In country lanes when young,
He knew the name of ev'ry bird
    But not the song it sung.

And when he could not hear me speak
    He smiled and looked so wise
That now I do not like to think
    Of maggots in his eyes.

He liked the rain-washed Cornish air
    And smell of ploughed-up soil,
He liked a landscape big and bare
    And painted it in oil.

But least of all he liked that place
    Which hangs on Highgate Hill
Of soaked Carrara-covered earth
    For Londoners to fill.

He would have liked to say good-bye,
    Shake hands with many friends,
In Highgate now his finger-bones
    Stick through his finger-ends.

You, God, who treat him thus and thus,
  Say 'Save his soul and pray.'
You ask me to believe You and
  I only see decay.

Parliament Hill Fields

Rumbling under lackened girders, Midland, bound for
   Cricklewood,
Puffed its sulphur to the sunset where that Land of Laundries
   stood.
Rumble under, thunder over, train and tram alternate go,
Shake the floor and smudge the ledger, Charrington, Sells,
   Dale and Co.,
Nuts and nuggets in the window, trucks along the lines below.

When the Bon Marché was shuttered, when the feet were hot
   and tired,
Outside Charrington's we waited, by the 'STOP HERE IF
   REQUIRED',
Launched aboard the shopping basket, sat precipitately down,
Rocked past Zwanziger the baker's, and the terrace blackish
   brown,
And the curious Anglo-Norman parish church of Kentish
   Town.

Till the tram went over thirty, sighting terminus again,
Past municipal lawn tennis and the bobble-hanging plane;
Soft the light suburban evening caught our ashlar-speckled
   spire,

Eighteen-sixty Early English, as the mighty elms retire
Either side of Brookfield Mansions flashing fine French-
   window fire.

Oh the after-tram-ride quiet, when we heard a mile beyond,
Silver music from the bandstand, barking dogs by Highgate
   Pond;

Up the hill where stucco houses in Virginia creeper down –
And my childish wave of pity, seeing children carrying down
Sheaves of drooping dandelions to the courts of Kentish Town.

A Subaltern's Love-song

Miss J. Hunter Dunn, Miss J. Hunter Dunn,
Furnish'd and burnish'd by Aldershot sun,
What strenuous singles we played after tea,
We in the tournament – you against me!

Love-thirty, love-forty, oh! weakness of joy,
The speed of a swallow, the grace of a boy,
With carefullest carelessness, gaily you won,
I am weak from your loveliness, Joan Hunter Dunn.

Miss Joan Hunter Dunn, Miss Joan Hunter Dunn,
How mad I am, sad I am, glad that you won.
The warm-handled racket is back in its press,
But my shock-headed victor, she loves me no less.

Her father's euonymus shines as we walk,
And swing past the summer-house, buried in talk,
And cool the verandah that welcomes us in
To the six-o'clock news and a lime-juice and gin.

The scent of the conifers, sound of the bath,
The view from my bedroom of moss-dappled path,
As I struggle with double-end evening tie,
For we dance at the Golf Club, my victor and I.

On the floor of her bedroom lie blazer and shorts
And the cream-coloured walls are be-trophied with sports,
And westering, questioning settles the sun
On your low-leaded window, Miss Joan Hunter Dunn.

The Hillman is waiting, the light's in the hall,
The pictures of Egypt are bright on the wall,
My sweet, I am standing beside the oak stair
And there on the landing's the light on your hair.

By roads 'not adopted', by woodlanded ways,
She drove to the club in the late summer haze,
Into nine-o'clock Camberley, heavy with bells
And mushroomy, pine-woody, evergreen smells.

Miss Joan Hunter Dunn, Miss Joan Hunter Dunn,
I can hear from the car-park the dance has begun.
Oh! full Surrey twilight! importunate band!
Oh! strongly adorable tennis-girl's hand!

Around us are Rovers and Austins afar,
Above us, the intimate roof of the car,
And here on my right is the girl of my choice,
With the tilt of her nose and the chime of her voice,

And the scent of her wrap, and the words never said,
And the ominous, ominous dancing ahead.
We sat in the car park till twenty to one
And now I'm engaged to Miss Joan Hunter Dunn.

Ireland with Emily

Bells are booming down the bohreens,
    White the mist along the grass.
Now the Julias, Maeves and Maureens
    Move between the fields to Mass.
Twisted trees of small green apple
Guard the decent whitewashed chapel,
Gilded gates and doorway grained
Pointed windows richly stained
    With many-coloured Munich glass.

See the black-shawled congregations
    On the broidered vestment gaze
Murmur past the painted stations
    As Thy Sacred Heart displays
Lush Kildare of scented meadows,
Roscommon, thin in ash-tree shadows,
And Westmeath the lake-reflected,
Spreading Leix the hill-protected,
    Kneeling all in silver haze!

In yews and woodbine, walls and guelder,
    Nettle-deep the faithful rest,
Winding leagues of flowering elder,
    Sycamore with ivy dressed,
Ruins in demesnes deserted,
Bog-surrounded bramble-skirted –
Townlands rich or townlands mean as
These, oh, counties of them screen us
    In the Kingdom of the West.

Stony seaboard, far and foreign,
    Stony hills poured over space,
Stony outcrop of the Burren,
    Stones in every fertile place,

Little fields with boulders dotted,
Grey-stone shoulders saffron-spotted,
Stone-walled cabins thatched with reeds,
Where a Stone Age people breeds
    The last of Europe's stone age race.

Has it held, the warm June weather?
    Draining shallow sea-pools dry,
    When we bicycled together
    Down the bohreens fuchsia-high.
Till there rose, abrupt and lonely,
A ruined abbey, chancel only,
Lichen-crusted, time-befriended,
Soared the arches, splayed and splendid,
    Romanesque against the sky.

There is pinnacled protection,
    One extinguished family waits
A Church of Ireland resurrection
    By the broken, rusty gates.
Sheepswool, straw and droppings cover,
Graves of spinster, rake and lover,
Whose fantastic mausoleum
Sings its own seablown Te Deum,
    In and out the slipping slates.

Margate, 1940

From out the Queen's Highcliffe for weeks at a stretch
I watched how the mower evaded the vetch,
So that over the putting-course rashes were seen
Of pink and of yellow among the burnt green.

How restful to putt, when the strains of a band
Announced a *thé dansant* was on at the Grand,
While over the privet, comminglingly clear,
I heard lesser 'Co-Optimists' down by the pier.

How lightly municipal, meltingly tarr'd,
Were the walks through the Laws by the Queen's Promenade
As soft over Cliftonville languished the light
Down Harold Road, Norfolk Road, into the night.

Oh! then what a pleasure to see the ground floor
With tables for two laid as tables for four,
And bottles of sauce and Kia-Ora* and squash
Awaiting their owners who'd gone up to wash –

Who had gone up to wash the ozone from their skins
The sand from their legs and the Rock from their chins,
To prepare for an evening of dancing and cards
And forget the sea-breeze on the dry promenades.

From third floor and fourth floor the children looked down
Upon ribbons of light in the salt-scented town;
And drowning the trams roared the sound of the sea
As it washed in the shingle the scraps of their tea.
* * *
Beside the Queen's Highcliffe now rank grows the vetch,
Now dark is the terrace, a storm-battered stretch;
And I think, as the fairy-lit sights I recall,
It is those we are fighting for, foremost of all.

* Pronounced 'Kee-ora'.

Invasion Exercise on the Poultry Farm

Softly croons the radiogram, loudly hoot the owls,
Judy gives the door a slam and goes to feed the fowls.
Marty rolls a Craven A around her ruby lips
And runs her yellow fingers down her corduroyded hips,
Shuts her mouth and screws her eyes and puffs her fag
    alight
And hears some most peculiar cries that echo through the
    night.

Ting-a-ling the telephone, to-whit to-whoo the owls,
Judy, Judy, Judy girl, and have you fed the fowls?
No answer as the poultry gate is swinging there ajar.
Boom the bombers overhead, between the clouds a star,
And just outside, among the arks, in a shadowy sheltered
    place

Lie Judy and a paratroop in horrible embrace.
Ting-a-ling the telephone. 'Yes, this is Marty Hayne.'
'Have you seen a paratroop come walking down your lane!
He may be on your premises, he may be somewhere near,
And if he is report the fact to Major Maxton-Weir.'
Marty moves in dread towards the window – standing there
Draws the curtain – sees the guilty movement of the pair.*
White with rage and lined with age but strong and sturdy
    still

Marty now co-ordinates her passions and her will,
She will teach that Judy girl to trifle with the heart
And go and kiss a paratroop like any common tart.
She switches up the radiogram and covered by the blare
She goes and gets a riding whip and whirls it in the air,
She fetches down a length of rope and rushes, breathing hard
To let the couple have it for embracing in the yard.
Crack! the pair are paralysed. Click! they cannot stir.

Zip! she's trussed the paratroop. There's no embracing *her*.
'Hullo, hullo, hullo, hullo . . . Major Maxton-Weir!
I've trussed your missing paratroop. He's waiting for you
here.'

* These lines in italic are by Henry Oscar.

In a Bath Teashop

'Let us not speak, for the love we bear one another –
    Let us hold hands and look.'
She, such a very ordinary little woman;
    He, such a thumping crook;
But both, for a moment, little lower than the angels
    In the teashop's ingle-nook.

Youth and Age on Beaulieu River, Hants

Early sun on Beaulieu water
    Lights the undersides of oaks,
Clumps of leaves it floods and blanches,
All transparent glow the branches
    Which the double sunlight soaks;
  To her craft on Beaulieu water
  Clemency the General's daughter
    Pulls across with even strokes.

Schoolboy-sure she is this morning;
    Soon her sharpie's rigg'd and free.
Cool beneath a garden awning
    Mrs. Fairclough, sipping tea
And raising large long-distance glasses
As the little sharpie passes,
    Sighs our sailor girl to see:

Tulip figure, so appealing,
    Oval face, so serious-eyed,
Tree-roots pass'd and muddy beaches.
On to huge and lake-like reaches,
    Soft and sun-warm, see her glide –
  Slacks the slim young limbs revealing,
  Sun-brown arm the tiller feeling –
    With the wind and with the tide.

Evening light will bring the water,
    Day-long sun will burst the bud,
Clemency, the General's daughter,
    Will return upon the flood.
But the older woman only
Knows the ebb-tide leaves her lonely
    With the shining fields of mud.

Indoor Games near Newbury

In among the silver birches winding ways of tarmac wander
   And the signs to Bussock Bottom, Tussock Wood and
      Windy Brake,
Gabled lodges, tile-hung churches, catch the lights of our
      Lagonda
   As we drive to Wendy's party, lemon curd and Christmas
   cake.

   Rich the makes of motor whirring,
   Past the pine-plantation purring
     Come up, Hupmobile, Delage!
   Short the way your chauffeurs travel,
   Crunching over private gravel
     Each from out his warm garáge.

Oh but Wendy, when the carpet yielded to my indoor pumps
   There you stood, your gold hair streaming,
   Handsome in the hall-light gleaming
There you looked and there you led me off into the game of
     clumps
   Then the new Victrola playing
   And your funny uncle saying
'Choose your partners for a fox-trot! Dance until its *tea*
   o'clock!
   'Come on, young 'uns, foot it featly!'
   Was it chance that paired us neatly,
   I, who loved you so completely,
You, who pressed me closely to you, hard against your party
   frock!

'Meet me when you've finished eating!' So we met and no one
   found us.
   Oh that dark and furry cupboard while the rest played hide
   and seek!

Holding hands our two hearts beating in the bedroom silence
     round us,
  Holding hands and hardly hearing sudden footstep, thud
    and shriek.

  Love that lay too deep for kissing –
  'Where *is* Wendy? Wendy's missing!'
    Love so pure it *had* to end,
  Love so strong that I was frighten'd
  When you gripped my fingers tight and
Hugging, whispered 'I'm your friend.'

Good-bye Wendy! Send the fairies, pinewood elf and larch
    tree gnome,
  Spingle-spangled stars are peeping
  At the lush Lagonda creeping
Down the winding ways of tarmac to the leaded lights of
    home.

  There, among the silver birches,
  All the bells of all the churches
Sounded in the bath-waste running out into the frosty air.
  Wendy speeded my undressing,
  Wendy is the sheet's caressing
  Wendy bending gives a blessing,
Holds me as I drift to dreamland, safe inside my
    slumber-wear.

from Beside the Seaside

Green Shutters, shut your shutters! Windyridge,
Let winds unnoticed whistle round your hill!
High Dormers, draw your curtains! Slam the door,
And pack the family in the Morris eight.
Lock up the garage. Put her in reverse,
Back out with care, now, forward, off – away!
The richer people living farther out
O'ertake us in their Rovers. We, in turn,
Pass poorer families hurrying on foot
Towards the station. Very soon the town
Will echo to the groan of empty trams
And sweetshops advertise Ice Cream in vain.
Solihull, Headingley and Golders Green.
Preston and Swindon, Manchester and Leeds,
Braintree and Bocking, hear the sea! the sea!
The smack of breakers upon windy rocks,
Spray blowing backwards from their curling walls
Of green translucent water. England leaves
Her centre for her tide-line. Father's toes,
Though now encased in coloured socks and shoes
And pressing the accelerator hard,
Ache for the feel of sand and little shrimps
To tickle in between them. Mother vows
To be more patient with the family:
Just for its sake she will be young again.
And, at that moment, Jennifer is sick
(Over-excitement must have brought it on,
The hurried breakfast and the early start)
And Michael's rather pale, and as for Anne . . .
'Please stop a moment, Hubert, anywhere.'
    So evening sunlight shows us Sandy Cove
The same as last year and the year before.
Still on the brick front of the Baptist Church

SIX-THIRTY. PREACHER :– *Mr Pentecost –*
All visitors are welcomed. Still the quartz
Glitters along the tops of garden walls.
Those macrocarpa still survive the gales
They must have had last winter. Still the shops
Remain unaltered on the Esplanade –
The Circulating Library, the Stores,
Jill's Pantry, Cynthia's Ditty Box (Antiques),
Trecarrow (Maps and Souvenirs and Guides).
Still on the terrace of the big hotel
Pale pink hydrangeas turn a rusty brown
Where sea winds catch them, and yet do not die.
The bumpy lane between the tamarisks,
The escallonia hedge, and still it's there –
Our lodging-house, ten minutes from the shore.
Still unprepared to make a picnic lunch
Except by notice on the previous day.
Still nowhere for the children when it's wet
Except that smelly, overcrowded lounge.
And still no garage for the motor-car.
Still on the bedroom wall, the list of rules:
Don't waste the water. It is pumped by hand.
Don't throw old blades into the W. C.
Don't keep the bathroom long and don't be late
For meals and don't hang swim-suits out on sills
(A line has been provided at the back).
Don't empty children's sand-shoes in the hall.
Don't this, Don't that. Ah, still the same, the same
As it was last year and the year before –
But rather more expensive, now, of course.

Christmas

The bells of waiting Advent ring,
    The Tortoise stove is lit again
And lamp-oil light across the night
    Has caught the streaks of winter rain
In many a stained-glass window sheen
From Crimson Lake to Hooker's Green.

The holly in the windy hedge
    And round the Manor House the yew
Will soon be stripped to deck the ledge,
    The altar, font and arch and pew,
So that the villagers can say
'The church looks nice' on Christmas Day.

Provincial public houses blaze
    And Corporation tramcars clang,
On lighted tenements I gaze
    Where paper decorations hang,
And bunting in the red Town Hall
Says 'Merry Christmas to you all.'

And London shops on Christmas Eve
    Are strung with silver bells and flowers
As hurrying clerks the City leave
    To pigeon-haunted classic towers,
And marbled clouds go scudding by
The many-steepled London sky.

And girls in slacks remember Dad,
    And oafish louts remember Mum,
And sleepless children's hearts are glad,
    And Christmas-morning bells say 'Come!'
Even to shining ones who dwell
Safe in the Dorchester Hotel.

And is it true? And is it true,
     This most tremendous tale of all,
Seen in a stained-glass window's hue,
     A Baby in an ox's stall?
The Maker of the stars and sea
Become a Child on earth for me?

And is it true? For if it is,
     No loving fingers tying strings
Around those tissued fripperies,
     The sweet and silly Christmas things,
Bath salts and inexpensive scent
And hideous tie so kindly meant,

No love that in a family dwells,
     No carolling in frosty air,
Nor all the steeple-shaking bells
     Can with this single Truth compare –
That God was Man in Palestine
And lives to-day in Bread and Wine.

The Licorice Fields at Pontefract

In the licorice fields at Pontefract
  My love and I did meet
And many a burdened licorice bush
  Was blooming round our feet;
Red hair she had and golden skin,
Her sulky lips were shaped for sin,
Her sturdy legs were flannel-slack'd,
The strongest legs in Pontefract.

The light and dangling licorice flowers
  Gave off the sweetest smells;
From various black Victorian towers
  The Sunday evening bells
Came pealing over dales and hills
And tanneries and silent mills
And lowly streets where country stops
And little shuttered corner shops.

She cast her blazing eyes on me
  And plucked a licorice leaf;
I was her captive slave and she
  My red-haired robber chief.
Oh love! for love I could not speak,
It left me winded, wilting, weak
And held in brown arms strong and bare
And wound with flaming ropes of hair.

House of Rest

Now all the world she knew is dead
    In this small room she lives her days
The wash-hand stand and single bed
    Screened from the public gaze.

The horse-brass shines, the kettle sings,
    The cup of China tea
Is tasted among cared-for things
    Ranged round for me to see –

Lincoln, by Valentine and Co.,
    Now yellowish brown and stained,
But there some fifty years ago
    Her Harry was ordained;

Outside the Church at Woodhall Spa
    The smiling groom and bride,
And here's his old tobacco jar
    Dried lavender inside.

I do not like to ask if he
    Was 'High' or 'Low' or 'Broad'
Lest such a question seem to be
    A mockery of Our Lord.

Her full grey eyes look far beyond
    The little room and me
To village church and village pond
    And ample rectory.

She sees her children each in place
    Eyes downcast as they wait,
She hears her Harry murmur Grace,
    Then heaps the porridge plate.

Aroused at seven, to bed by ten,
    They fully lived each day,
Dead sons, so motor-bike-mad then,
    And daughters far away.

Now when the bells for Eucharist
    Sound in the Market Square,
With sunshine struggling through the mist
    And Sunday in the air,

The veil between her and her dead
    Dissolves and shows them clear,
The Consecration Prayer is said
    And all of them are near.

Middlesex

Gaily into Ruislip Gardens
 Runs the red electric train,
With a thousand Ta's and Pardon's
 Daintily alights Elaine;
Hurries down the concrete station
With a frown of concentration,
Out into the outskirt's edges
Where a few surviving hedges
Keep alive our lost Elysium – rural Middlesex again.

Well cut Windsmoor flapping lightly,
 Jacqmar scarf of mauve and green
Hiding hair which, Friday nightly,
 Delicately drowns in Drene;
Fair Elaine the bobby-soxer,
Fresh-complexioned with Innoxa,
Gains the garden – father's hobby –
Hangs her Windsmoor in the lobby,
Settles down to sandwich supper and the television screen.

Gentle Brent, I used to know you
 Wandering Wembley-wards at will,
Now what change your waters show you
 In the meadowlands you fill!
Recollect the elm-trees misty
And the footpaths climbing twisty
Under cedar-shaded palings,
Low laburnum-leaned-on railings,
Out of Northolt on and upward to the heights of Harrow hill.

Parish of enormous hayfields
 Perivale stood all alone,
And from Greenford scent of mayfields
 Most enticingly was blown

Over market gardens tidy,
Taverns for the *bona fide*,
Cockney anglers, cockney shooters,
Murray Poshes, Lupin Pooters
Long in Kensal Green and Highgate silent under soot and
stone.

Norfolk

How did the Devil come? When first attack?
  These Norfolk lanes recall lost innocence,
The years fall off and find me walking back
  Dragging a stick along the wooden fence
Down this same path, where, forty years ago,
My father strolled behind me, calm and slow.

I used to fill my hand with sorrel seeds
  And shower him with them from the tops of stiles,
I used to butt my head into his tweeds
  To make him hurry down those languorous miles
Of ash and alder-shaded lanes, till here
Our moorings and the masthead would appear.

There after supper lit by lantern light
  Warm in the cabin I could lie secure
And hear against the polished sides at night
  The lap lap lapping of the weedy Bure,
A whispering and watery Norfolk sound
Telling of all the moonlit reeds around.

How did the Devil come? When first attack?
  The church is just the same, though now I know
Fowler of Louth restored it. Time, bring back
  The rapturous ignorance of long ago,
The peace, before the dreadful daylight starts,
Of unkept promises and broken hearts.

The Metropolitan Railway
Baker Street Station Buffet

Early Electric! With what radiant hope
   Men formed this many-branched electrolier,
Twisted the flex around the iron rope
   And let the dazzling vacuum globes hang clear,
And then with hearts the rich contrivance fill'd
Of copper, beaten by the Bromsgrove Guild.

Early Electric! Sit you down and see,
   'Mid this fine woodwork and a smell of dinner,
A stained-glass windmill and a pot of tea,
   And sepia views of leafy lanes in PINNER, –
Then visualize, far down the shining lines,
Your parents' homestead set in murmuring pines.

Smoothly from HARROW, passing PRESTON ROAD,
   They saw the last green fields and misty sky,
At NEASDEN watched a workmen's train unload,
   And, with the morning villas sliding by,
They felt so sure on their electric trip
That Youth and Progress were in partnership.

And all that day in murky London Wall
   The thought of RUISLIP kept him warm inside;
At FARRINGDON that lunch hour at a stall
   He bought a dozen plants of London Pride;
While she, in arc-lit Oxford Street adrift,
Soared through the sales by safe hydraulic lift.

Early Electric! Maybe even here
   They met that evening at six-fifteen
Beneath the hearts of this electrolier
   And caught the first non-stop to WILLESDEN GREEN,
Then out and on, through rural RAYNER'S LANE
To autumn-scented Middlesex again.

Cancer has killed him. Heart is killing her.
    The trees are down.   An Odeon flashes fire
Where stood their villa by the murmuring fir
    When 'they would for their children's good conspire.'
Of their loves and hopes on hurrying feet
Thou art the worn memorial, Baker Street.

Late-Flowering Lust

My head is bald, my breath is bad,
    Unshaven is my chin,
I have not now the joys I had
    When I was young in sin.

I run my fingers down your dress
    With brandy-certain aim
And you respond to my caress
    And maybe feel the same.

But I've a picture of my own
    On this reunion night,
Wherein two skeletons are shewn
    To hold each other tight;

Dark sockets look on emptiness
    Which once was loving-eyed,
The mouth that opens for a kiss
    Has got no tongue inside.

I cling to you inflamed with fear
    As now you cling to me,
I feel how frail you are my dear
    And wonder what will be –

A week? or twenty years remain?
    And then – what kind of death?
A losing fight with frightful pain
    Or a gasping fight for breath?

Too long we let our bodies cling,
    We cannot hide disgust
At all the thoughts that in us spring
    From this late-flowering lust.

Sun and Fun

Song of a Night-club Proprietress

I walked into the night-club in the morning;
    There was kummel on the handle of the door.
The ashtrays were unemptied,
The cleaning unattempted,
    And a squashed tomato sandwich on the floor.

I pulled aside the thick magenta curtains
    – So Regency, so Regency, my dear –
And a host of little spiders
Ran a race across the ciders
    To a box of baby 'pollies by the beer.

Oh sun upon the summer-going by-pass
    Where ev'rything is speeding to the sea,
And wonder beyond wonder
That here where lorries thunder
    The sun should ever percolate to me.

When Boris used to call in his Sedanca,
    When Teddy took me down to his estate
When my nose excited passion,
When my clothes were in the fashion,
    When my beaux were never cross if I was late,

There was sun enough for lazing upon beaches,
    There was fun enough for far into the night.
But I'm dying now and done for,
What on earth was all the fun for?
    For I'm old and ill and terrified and tight.

Original Sin on the Sussex Coast

Now on this out of season afternoon
Day schools which cater for the sort of boy
Whose parents go by Pullman once a month
To do a show in town, pour out their young
Into the sharply red October light.
Here where The Drive and Buckhurst Road converge
I watch the rival gangs and am myself
A schoolboy once again in shivering shorts.
I see the dust of sherbet on the chin
Of Andrew Knox well-dress'd, well-born, well-fed,
Even at nine a perfect gentleman,
Willie Buchanan waiting at his side –
Another Scot, eruptions on his skin.
I hear Jack Drayton whistling from the fence
Which hides the copper domes of 'Cooch Behar'.
That was the signal. So there's no escape.
A race for Willow Way and jump the hedge
Behind the Granville Bowling Club? Too late.
They'll catch me coming out in Seapink Lane.
Across the Garden of Remembrance? No,
That would be blasphemy and bring bad luck.
Well then, I'm *for* it. Andrew's at me first,
He pinions me in that especial grip
His brother learned in Kobë from a Jap
(No chance for me against the Japanese).
Willie arrives and winds me with a punch
Plum in the tummy, grips the other arm.
'You're to be booted. Hold him steady, chaps!'
A wait for taking aim. Oh trees and sky!
Then crack against the column of my spine,
Blackness and breathlessness and sick with pain
I stumble on the asphalt. Off they go
Away, away, thank God, and out of sight

So that I lie quite still and climb to sense
Too out of breath and strength to make a sound.
   Now over Polegate vastly sets the sun;
Dark rise the Downs from darker looking elms,
And out of Southern railway trains to tea
Run happy boys down various Station Roads,
Satchels of homework jogging on their backs,
So trivial and so healthy in the shade
Of these enormous Downs. And when they're home,
When the Post-Toasties mixed with Golden Shred
Make for the kiddies such a scrumptious feast,
Does Mum, the Persil-user, still believe
That there's no Devil and that youth is bliss?
As certain as the sun behind the Downs
And quite as plain to see, the Devil walks.

Devonshire Street W.1

The heavy mahogany door with its wrought-iron screen
   Shuts. And the sound is rich, sympathetic, discreet.
The sun still shines on this eighteenth-century scene
   With Edwardian faience adornments – Devonshire Street

No hope. And the X-ray photographs under his arm
   Confirm the message. His wife stands timidly by.
The opposite brick-built house looks lofty and calm
   Its chimneys steady against a mackerel sky.

No hope. And the iron nob of this palisade
   So cold to the touch, is luckier now than he
'Oh merciless, hurrying Londoners! Why was I made
   For the long and the painful deathbed coming to me?'

She puts her fingers in his as, loving and silly,
   At long-past Kensington dances she used to do
'It's cheapter to take the tube to Piccadilly
   And then we can catch a nineteen or a twenty-two.'

The Cottage Hospital

At the end of a long-walled garden
    in a red provincial town,
A brick path led to a mulberry –
    scanty grass at its feet.
I lay under blackening branches
    where the mulberry leaves hung down
Sheltering ruby fruit globes
    from a Sunday-tea-time heat.
Apple and plum espaliers
    basked upon bricks of brown;
The air was swimming with insects,
    and children played in the street.

Out of this bright intentness
    into the mulberry shade
Musca domestica (housefly)
    swung from the August light
Slap into slithery rigging
    by the waiting spider made
Which spun the lithe elastic
    till the fly was shrouded tight.
Down came the hairy talons
    and horrible poison blade
And none of the garden noticed
    that fizzing, hopeless fight.

Say in what Cottage Hospital
    whose pale green walls resound
With the tap upon polished parquet
    of inflexible nurses' feet
Shall I myself be lying
    when they range the screens around?
And say shall I groan in dying,
    as I twist the sweaty sheet?

Or gasp for breath uncrying,
   as I feel my senses drown'd
While the air is swimming with insects
   and children play in the street?

Business Girls

From the geyser ventilators
  Autumn winds are blowing down
On a thousand business women
  Having baths in Camden Town.

Waste pipes chuckle into runnels,
  Steam's escaping here and there,
Morning trains through Camden cutting
  Shake the Crescent and the Square.

Early nip of changeful autumn,
  Dahlias glimpsed through garden doors,
At the back precarious bathrooms
  Jutting out from upper floors;

And behind their frail partitions
  Business women lie and soak,
Seeing through the draughty skylight
  Flying clouds and railway smoke.

Rest you there, poor unbelov'd ones,
  Lap your loneliness in heat.
All too soon the tiny breakfast,
  Trolley-bus and windy street!

Hunter Trials

It's awf'lly bad luck on Diana,
    Her ponies have swallowed their bits;
She fished down their throats with a spanner
    And frightened them all into fits.

So now she's attempting to borrow.
    Do lend her some bits, Mummy, *do*;
I'll lend her my own for to-morrow,
    But to-day *I*'ll be wanting them too.

Just look at Prunella on Guzzle,
    The wizardest pony on earth;
Why doesn't she slacken his muzzle
    And tighten the breech in his girth?

I say, Mummy, there's Mrs. Geyser
    And doesn't she look pretty sick?
I bet it's because Mona Lisa
    Was hit on the hock with a brick.

Miss Blewitt says Monica threw it,
    But Monica says it was Joan,
And Joan's very thick with Miss Blewitt,
    So Monica's sulking alone.

And Margaret failed in her paces,
    Her withers got tied in a noose,
So her coronets caught in the traces
    And now all her fetlocks are loose.

Oh, it's me now. I'm terribly nervous.
    I wonder if Smudges will shy.
She's practically certain to swerve as
    Her Pelham is over one eye.

        *   *   *

Oh wasn't it naughty of Smudges?
    Oh, Mummy, I'm sick with disgust.
She threw me in front of the Judges,
    And my silly old collarbone's bust.

How to Get On in Society
Originally set as a competition in 'Time and Tide'

Phone for the fish-knives, Norman
    As Cook is a little unnerved;
You kiddies have crumpled the serviettes
    And I must have things daintily served.

Are the requisites all in the toilet?
    The frills round the cutlets can wait
Till the girl has replenished the cruets
    And switched on the logs in the grate.

It's ever so close in the lounge, dear,
    But the vestibule's comfy for tea
And Howard is out riding on horseback
    So do come and take some with me.

Now here is a fork for your pastries
    And do use the couch for your feet;
I know what I wanted to ask you –
    Is trifle sufficient for sweet?

Milk and then just as it comes dear?
    I'm afraid the preserve's full of stones;
Beg pardon, I'm soiling the doileys
    With afternoon tea-cakes and scones.

Winthrop Mackworth Redivivus

It's for Regency now I'm enthusing
 So we've Regency stripes on the wall
And – my dear, really frightf'lly amusing –
 A dome of wax fruit in the hall.
We've put the Van Gogh in the bathroom,
 Those sunflowers looked *so* out of date,
But instead, as there's plenty of hearth room,
 Real ivy grows out of the grate.

And plants for indoors are the fashion –
 Or so the *News Chronicle* said –
So I've ventured some housekeeping cash on
 A cactus which seems to be dead.
An artist with whom we're acquainted
 Has stippled the dining-room stove
And the walls are alternately painted
 Off-yellow and festival mauve.

The Minister's made the decision
 That Cedric's department must stay
So an O.B.E. (Civil Division)
 Will shortly be coming his way.
To you, dear, and also to me, dear,
 It's nothing, for you are a friend,
Not even if you and I see, dear,
 A knighthood, perhaps, in the end.

But it wasn't for this that I fill'd a
 Whole page up with gossip of course.
No: I'm dreadf'lly concerned for Matilda
 Who seems to believe she's a horse.
She neighs when we're sitting at table
 And clutches a make-believe rein.

Her playroom she fancies a stable.
    Do you think she is going insane?

I know I would not let them christen her –
    Such an old superstition's absurd –
But when Cedric was reading *The Listener*
    Before he tuned in to the Third,
She walked on all fours like a dumb thing
    And nibbled my plants, I'm afraid.
Do you think we could exorcize something
    If we called in the Church to our aid?

Ex-horse-ize – that's rather funny –
    But it's not very funny to me
For I've spent all her grandmother's money
    On analysis since she was three.
And just when we'd freed her libido
    We went off to Venice and Rome
(You'll remember we met on the Lido)
    And left dear Matilda at home.

I'm afraid that that Riding School did it,
    The one where we sent her to stay;
Were she horse-mad before, then she hid it
    Or her analyst kept it at bay.
But that capable woman in Surrey
    Who seemed so reliable too,
Said 'Leave her to me and don't worry,
    This place is as good as the Zoo.

When she's not on a horse she's not idle;
    She can muck out the stables and clean
Her snaffle and saddle and bridle
    Till bed-time at seven-fifteen.'
Twenty guineas a week was the price, dear,
    For Matilda it may have been bliss,
But for us it is not very nice, dear,
    To find it has left her like this.

False Security

I remember the dread with which I at a quarter past four
Let go with a bang behind me our house front door
And, clutching a present for my dear little hostess tight,
Sailed out for the children's party into the night
Or rather the gathering night. For still some boys
In the near municipal acres were making a noise
Shuffling in fallen leaves and shouting and whistling
And running past hedges of hawthorn, spikey and bristling.
And black in the oncoming darkness stood out the trees
And pink shone the ponds in the sunset ready to freeze
And all was still and ominous waiting for dark
And the keeper was ringing his closing bell in the park
And the arc lights started to fizzle and burst into mauve
As I climbed West Hill to the great big house in The Grove,
Where the children's party was and the dear little hostess.
But halfway up stood the empty house where the ghost is
I crossed to the other side and under the arc
Made a rush for the next kind lamp-post out of the dark
And so to the next and the next till I reached the top
Where the Grove branched off to the left. Then ready
    to drop
I ran to the ironwork gateway of number seven
Secure at last on the lamplit fringe of Heaven.
Oh who can say how subtle and safe one feels
Shod in one's children's sandals from Daniel Neal's,
Clad in one's party clothes made of stuff from Heal's?
And who can still one's thrill at the candle shine
On cakes and ices and jelly and blackcurrant wine,
And the warm little feel of my hostess's hand in mine?
Can I forget my delight at the conjuring show?
And wasn't I proud that I was the last to go?
Too overexcited and pleased with myself to know
That the words I heard my hostess's mother employ

To a guest departing, would ever diminish my joy,
I WONDER WHERE JULIA FOUND THAT STRANGE, RATHER
  COMMON LITTLE BOY?

Eunice

With her latest roses happily encumbered
    Tunbridge Wells Central takes her from the night,
Sweet second bloomings frost has faintly umbered
    And some double dahlias waxy red and white.

Shut again till April stands her little hutment
    Peeping over daisies Michaelmas and mauve,
Lock'd is the Elsan in its brick abutment
    Lock'd the little pantry, dead the little stove.

Keys with Mr Groombridge, but nobody will take them
    To her lonely cottage by the lonely oak,
Potatoes in the garden but nobody to bake them,
    Fungus in the living room and water in the coke.

I can see her waiting on this chilly Sunday
    For the five forty (twenty minutes late),
One of many hundreds to dread the coming Monday
    To fight with influenza and battle with her weight.

Tweed coat and skirt that with such anticipation
    On a merry spring time a friend had trimm'd with fur,
Now the friend is married and, oh desolation,
    Married to the man who might have married *her*.

High in Onslow Gardens where the soot flakes settle
    An empty flat is waiting her struggle up the stair
And when she puts the wireless on, the heater and the kettle
    It's cream and green and cosy, but home is never there.

Home's here in Kent and how many morning coffees
    And hurried little lunch hours of planning will be spent
Through the busy months of typing in the office
    Until the days are warm enough to take her back to Kent.

Felixstowe, or The Last of Her Order

With one consuming roar along the shingle
   The long wave claws and rakes the pebbles down
To where its backwash and the next wave mingle,
   A mounting arch of water weedy-brown
Against the tide the off-shore breezes blow.
Oh wind and water, this is Felixstowe.

In winter when the sea winds chill and shriller
   Than those of summer, all their cold unload
Full on the gimcrack attic of the villa
   Where I am lodging off the Orwell Road,
I put my final shilling in the meter
And only make my loneliness completer.

In eighteen ninety-four when we were founded,
   Counting our Reverend Mother we were six,
How full of hope we were and prayer-surrounded
   'The Little Sisters of the Hanging Pyx'.
We built our orphanage. We ran our school.
Now only I am left to keep the rule.

Here in the gardens of the Spa Pavilion
   Warm in the whisper of a summer sea,
The cushioned scabious, a deep vermilion,
   With white pins stuck in it, looks up at me
A sun-lit kingdom touched by butterflies
And so my memory of winter dies.

Across the grass the poplar shades grow longer
   And louder clang the waves along the coast.
The band packs up. The evening breeze is stronger
   And all the world goes home to tea and toast.
I hurry past a cakeshop's tempting scones
Bound for the red brick twilight of St John's.

'Thou knowest my down sitting and mine uprising'
   Here where the white light burns with steady glow
Safe from the vain world's silly sympathizing,
   Safe with the Love that I was born to know,
Safe from the surging of the lonely sea
My heart finds rest, my heart finds rest in Thee.

Pershore Station, or A Liverish Journey First Class

The train at Pershore station was waiting that Sunday night
Gas light on the platform, in my carriage electric light,
Gas light on frosty evergreens, electric on Empire wood,
The Victorian world and the present in a moment's neigh-
    bourhood.

There was no one about but a conscript who was saying good-
    bye to his love
On the windy weedy platform with the sprinkled stars above
When sudden the waiting stillness shook with the ancient
    spells
Of an older world than all our worlds in the sound of the
    Pershore bells.

They were ringing them down for Evensong in the lighted
    abbey near,
Sounds which had poured through apple boughs for seven
    centuries here.
With Guilt, Remorse, Eternity the void within me fills
And I thought of her left behind me in the Herefordshire hills.

I remembered her defencelessness as I made my heart a stone
Till she wove her self-protection round and left me on my
    own.
And plunged in a deep self pity I dreamed of another wife
And lusted for freckled faces and lived a separate life.

One word would have made her love me, one word would
    have made her turn.
But the word I never murmured and now I am left to burn.
Evesham, Oxford and London. The carriage is new and smart.
I am cushioned and soft and heated with a deadweight in my
    heart.

Hertfordshire

I had forgotten Hertfordshire,
　　The large unwelcome fields of roots
Where with my knickerbockered sire
　　I trudged in syndicated shoots;

And that unlucky day when I
　　Fired by mistake into the ground
Under a Lionel Edwards sky
　　And felt disapprobation round.

The slow drive home by motor-car,
　　A heavy Rover Landaulette,
Through Welwyn, Hatfield, Potters Bar,
　　Tweed and cigar smoke, gloom and wet:

'How many times must I explain
　　The way a boy should hold a gun?'
I recollect my father's pain
　　At such a milksop for a son.

And now I see these fields once more
　　Clothed, thank the Lord, in summer green,
Pale corn waves rippling to a shore
　　The shadowy cliffs of elm between,

Colour-washed cottages reed-thatched
　　And weather-boarded water mills,
Flint churches, brick and plaster patched,
　　On mildly undistinguished hills –

They still are there. But now the shire
　　Suffers a devastating change,
Its gentle landscape strung with wire,
　　Old places looking ill and strange.

One can't be sure where London ends,
　　New towns have filled the fields of root

Where father and his business friends
　　Drove in the Landaulette to shoot;

Tall concrete standards line the lane,
　　Brick boxes glitter in the sun:
Far more would these have caused him pain
　　Than my mishandling of a gun.

Inevitable

First there was putting hot-water bottles to it,
　　Then there was seeing what an osteopath could do,
Then trying drugs to coax the thing and woo it,
　　Then came the time when he knew that he was through.

Now in his hospital bed I see him lying
　　Limp on the pillows like a cast-off Teddy bear.
Is he too ill to know that he is dying?
　　And, if he does know, does he really care?

Grey looks the ward with November's overcasting
　　But his large eyes seem to see beyond the day;
Speech becomes sacred near silence everlasting
　　Oh if I *must* speak, have I words to say?

In the past weeks we had talked about Variety,
　　Vesta Victoria, Lew Lake and Wilkie Bard,
Horse-buses, hansoms, crimes in High Society –
　　Although we knew his death was near, we fought against it
　　　　hard

Now from his remoteness in a stillness unaccountable
　　He drags himself to earth again to say good-bye to me –
His final generosity when almost insurmountable
　　The barriers and mountains he has crossed again must be.

N.W.5 & N.6

Red cliffs arise. And up them service lifts
Soar with the groceries to silver heights.
Lissenden Mansions. And my memory sifts
Lilies from lily-like electric lights
And Irish stew smells from the smell of prams
And roar of seas from roar of London trams.

Out of it all my memory carves the quiet
Of that dark privet hedge where pleasures breed,
There first, intent upon its leafy diet,
I watched the looping caterpillar feed
And saw it hanging in a gummy froth
Till, weeks on, from the chrysalis burst the moth.

I see black oak twigs outlined on the sky,
Red squirrels on the Burdett-Coutts estate.
I ask my nurse the question 'Will I die?'
As bells from sad St Anne's ring out so late,
'And if I do die, will I go to Heaven?'
Highgate at eventide. Nineteen-eleven.

'You will. I won't.' From that cheap nursery-maid,
Sadist and puritan as now I see,
I first learned what it was to be afraid,
Forcibly fed when sprawled across her knee
Lock'd into cupboards, left alone all day,
'World without end.' What fearsome words to pray.

'World without end.' It was not what she'ld do
That frightened me so much as did her fear
And guilt at endlessness. I caught them too,
Hating to think of sphere succeeding sphere
Into eternity and God's dread will.
I caught her terror then. I have it still.

from Summoned by Bells
Chapter III: Highgate

O Peggy Purey-Cust, how pure you were:
My first and purest love, Miss Purey-Cust!
Satchel on back I hurried up West Hill
To catch you on your morning walk to school,
Your nanny with you and your golden hair
Streaming like sunlight. Strict deportment made
You hold yourself erect and every step
Bounced up and down as though you walked on springs.
Your ice-blue eyes, your lashes long and light,
Your sweetly freckled face and turned-up nose
So haunted me that all my loves since then
Have had a look of Peggy Purey-Cust.
Along the Grove, what happy, happy steps
Under the limes I took to Byron House,
And blob-work, weaving, carpentry and art,
Walking with you; and with what joy returned.
Wendy you were to me in *Peter Pan*,
The Little Match Girl in Hans Andersen –
But I would rescue you before you died.
And once you asked me to your house to tea:
It seemed a palace after 31 –
The lofty entrance hall, the flights of stairs,
The huge expanse of sunny drawing-room,
Looking for miles across the chimney-pots
To spired St Pancras and the dome of Paul's;
And there your mother from a sofa smiled.
After that tea I called and called again,
But Peggy was not in. She was away;
She wasn't well. *House of the Sleeping Winds*,
My favourite book with whirling art-nouveau
And Walter Crane-ish colour plates, I brought
To cheer her sick-bed. It was taken in.

74

Weeks passed and passed . . . and then it was returned.
Oh gone for ever, Peggy Purey-Cust!

And at that happy school in Byron House
Only one harbinger of future woe
Came to me in those far, sun-gilded days –
Gold with the hair of Peggy Purey-Cust –
Two other boys (my rivals, I suppose)
Came suddenly round a corner, caught my arms
And one, a treacherous, stocky little Scot,
Winded me with a punch and "Want some more?"
He grunted when I couldn't speak for pain.
Why did he do it? Why that other boy,
Who hitherto had been a friend of mine,
Was his accomplice I could not divine,
Nor ever have done. But those fatal two
Continued with me to another school –
Avernus by the side of Highgate Hill.

Let those who have such memories recollect
Their sinking dread of going back to school.
I well remember mine. I see again
The great headmaster's study lined with books
Where somewhere, in a corner, there were canes.
He wrapped his gown, the great headmaster did,
About himself, chucked off his mortar-board
And, leaning back, said: 'Let's see what you know,
How many half-crowns are there in a pound?'
I didn't know. I couldn't even guess.
My poor fond father, hearing nothing, smiled;
The gold clock ticked; the waiting furniture
Shone like a colour plate by H. M. Brock . . .
No answer – and the great headmaster frown'd;
But let me in to Highgate Junior School.

In late September, in the conker time,
When Poperinghe and Zillebeke and Mons
Boomed with five-nines, large sepia gravures
Of French, Smith-Dorrien and Haig were given

Gratis with each half-pound of Brooke Bond's tea.
A neighbour's son had just been killed at Ypres;
Another had been wounded. *Rainbow* came
On Wednesdays – with the pranks of Tiger Tim,
And Bonnie Bluebell and her magic gloves.
'Your Country needs you!' serious Kitchener
Commanded from the posters. Up West Hill
I walked red-capped and jacketed to school,
A new boy much too early: school at nine,
And here I was outside at half-past eight.
I see the asphalt slope and smell again
The sluggish, sour, inadequate latrines.
I watch the shrubbery shake as, leaping out,
Come my two enemies of Byron House,
But now red-capped and jacketed like me:

> 'Betjeman's a German spy –
> Shoot him down and let him die:
> Betjeman's a German spy,
> A German spy, a German spy.'

They danced around me and their merry shouts
Brought other merry newcomers to see.
    Walking from school is a consummate art:
Which routes to follow to avoid the gangs,
Which paths to find that lead, circuitous,
To leafy squirrel haunts and plopping ponds,
For dreams of Archibald and Tiger Tim;
Which hiding-place is safe, and when it is;
What time to leave to dodge the enemy.
I only once was trapped. I knew the trap –
I heard it in their tones: 'Walk back with us.'
I knew they weren't my friends; but that soft voice
Wheedled me from my route to cold Swain's Lane.
There in a holly bush they threw me down,
Pulled off my shorts, and laughed and ran away;
And, as I struggled up, I saw grey brick,

The cemetery railings and the tombs.

  See the rich elms careering down the hill –
Full billows rolling into Holloway;
In the tall classroom hear again the drone
Of multiplication tables chanted out;
Recall how Kelly stood us in a ring:
'Three sevens, then add eight, and take away
Twelve; what's the answer?' Hesitation then
Meant shaking by the shoulders till we cried.
Deal out again the dog-eared poetry books
Where Hemans, Campbell, Longfellow and Scott
Mixed their dim lights with Edgar Allan Poe
(Who 'died of dissipation', said the notes).
'And what is dissipation, please, Miss Long?'
Its dreadfulness so pleased me that I learned
'The Bells' by heart, but all the time preferred
'Casablanca' and 'The Hesperus'
As poetry, and Campbell's 'Soldier's Dream'.
I couldn't see why Shakespeare was admired;
I thought myself as good as Campbell now
And very nearly up to Longfellow;
And so I bound my verse into a book,
The Best of Betjeman, and handed it
To one who, I was told, liked poetry –
The American master, Mr Eliot.
That dear good man, with Prufrock in his head
And Sweeney waiting to be agonized,
I wonder what he thought? He never says
When now we meet, across the port and cheese.
He looks the same as then, long, lean and pale,
Still with the slow deliberating speech
And enigmatic answers. At the time
A boy called Jelly said 'He thinks they're bad' –
But he himself is still too kind to say.

Preface to 'High and Low'

MURRAY, you bid my plastic pen
A preface write. Well, here's one then.
Verse seems to me the shortest way
Of saying what one has to say,
A memorable means of dealing
With mood or person, place or feeling.
Anything extra that is given
Is taken as a gift from Heaven.

The English language has such range,
Such rhymes and half-rhymes, rhythms strange,
And such variety of tone,
It is a music of its own.
With MILTON it has organ power
As loud as bells in Redcliffe tower;
It falls like winter crisp and light
On COWPER's Buckinghamshire night.
It can be gentle as a lake,
Where WORDSWORTH's oars a ripple make
Or rest with TENNYSON at ease
In sibilance of summer seas,
Or languorous as lilies grow,
When DOWSON's lamp is burning low –
For endless changes can be rung
On church-bells of the English tongue.

MURRAY, your venerable door
Opened to BYRON, CRABBE and MOORE
And TOMMY CAMPBELL. How can I,
A buzzing insubstantial fly,
Compare with them? I do not try,
Pleased simply to be one who shares
An imprint that was also theirs,
And grateful to the people who
Have bought my verses hitherto.

Tregardock

A mist that from the moor arose
   In sea-fog wraps Port Isaac bay,
The moan of warning from Trevose
   Makes grimmer this October day.

Only the shore and cliffs are clear.
   Gigantic slithering shelves of slate
In waiting awfulness appear
   Like journalism full of hate.

On the steep path a bramble leaf
   Stands motionless and wet with dew,
The grass bends down, the bracken's brown,
   The grey-green gorse alone is new.

Cautious my sliding footsteps go
   To quarried rock and dripping cave;
The ocean, leaden-still below,
   Hardly has strength to lift a wave.

I watch it crisp into its height
   And flap exhausted on the beach,
The long surf menacing and white
   Hissing as far as it can reach.

The dunlin do not move, each bird
   Is stationary on the sand
As if a spirit in it heard
   The final end of sea and land.

And I on my volcano edge
   Exposed to ridicule and hate
Still do not dare to leap the ledge
   And smash to pieces on the slate.

Great Central Railway
Sheffield Victoria to Banbury

'Unmitigated England'
   Came swinging down the line
That day the February sun
   Did crisp and crystal shine.
Dark red at Kirkby Bentinck stood
   A steeply gabled farm
'Mid ash trees and a sycamore
   In charismatic calm.
A village street – a manor house –
   A church – then, tally ho!
We pounded through a housing scheme
   With tellymasts a-row,
Where cars of parked executives
   Did regimented wait
Beside administrative blocks
   Within the factory gate.
She waved to us from Hucknall South
   As we hooted round a bend,
From a curtained front-room window did
   The diesel driver's friend.
Through cuttings deep to Nottingham
   Precariously we wound;
The swallowing tunnel made the train
   Seem London's Underground.
Above the fields of Leicestershire
   On arches we were borne
And the rumble of the railway drowned
   The thunder of the Quorn;
And silver shone the steeples out
   Above the barren boughs;
Colts in a paddock ran from us
   But not the solid cows;

And quite where Rugby Central is
    Does only Rugby know.
We watched the empty platform wait
    And sadly saw it go.
By now the sun of afternoon
    Showed ridge and furrow shadows
And shallow unfamiliar lakes
    Stood shivering in the meadows.
Is Woodford church or Hinton church
    The one I ought to see?
Or were they both too much restored
    In 1883!
I do not know. Towards the west
    A trail of glory runs
And we leave the old Great Central line
    For Banbury and buns.

Five o'Clock Shadow

This is the time of day when we in the Men's Ward
  Think 'One more surge of the pain and I give up the fight,'
When he who struggles for breath can struggle less strongly:
  This is the time of day which is worse than night.

A haze of thunder hangs on the hospital rose-beds,
  A doctors' foursome out on the links is played,
Safe in her sitting-room Sister is putting her feet up:
  This is the time of day when we feel betrayed.

Below the windows, loads of loving relations
  Rev in the car park, changing gear at the bend,
Making for home and a nice big tea and the telly:
  'Well, we've done what we can. It can't be long till the end.'

This is the time of day when the weight of bedclothes
  Is harder to bear than a sharp incision of steel.
The endless anonymous croak of a cheap transistor
  Intensifies the lonely terror I feel.

The Cockney Amorist

Oh when my love, my darling,
    You've left me here alone,
I'll walk the streets of London
    Which once seemed all our own.

The vast suburban churches
    Together we have found:
The ones which smelt of gaslight
    The ones in incense drown'd;
I'll use them now for praying in
    And not for looking round.

No more the Hackney Empire
    Shall find us in its stalls
When on the limelit crooner
    The thankful curtain falls,
And soft electric lamplight
    Reveals the gilded walls.

I will not go to Finsbury Park
    The putting course to see
Nor cross the crowded High Road
    To Williamsons' to tea,
For these and all the other things
    Were part of you and me.

I love you, oh my darling,
    And what I can't make out
Is why since you have left me
    I'm somehow still about.

Reproof Deserved, or After the Lecture

When I saw the grapefruit drying, cherry in each centre lying,
   And a dozen guests expected at the table's polished oak,
Then I knew, my lecture finished, I'ld be feeling quite
      diminished
   Talking on, but unprotected, so that all my spirit broke.

'Have you read the last Charles Morgan?' 'Are you writing for
   the organ
   Which is published as a vital adjunct to our cultural
   groups?'
'This year some of us are learning all *The Lady's Not for*
    Burning
   For a poetry recital we are giving to the troops.'

'Mr Betjeman, I grovel before critics of the novel,
   Tell me, if I don't offend you, have you written one your
   self?
You haven't? Then the one I wrote is (not that I expect a
   notice)
   Something I would like to send you, just for keeping on
   your self.'

'Betjeman, I bet your racket brings you in a pretty packet
   Raising the old lecture curtain, writing titbits here and
   there.
But, by Jove, your hair is thinner, since you came to us in
   Pinner,
   And you're fatter now, I'm certain. What you need is
   country air.'

This and that way conversation, till I turn in desperation
   To a kind face (can I doubt it?) mercifully mute so far.
'Oh,' it says, 'I missed the lecture, wasn't it on architecture?
   Do please tell me all about it, what you do and who
   you are.'

Aldershot Crematorium

Between the swimming-pool and cricket-ground
    How straight the crematorium driveway lies!
And little puffs of smoke without a sound
    Show what we loved dissolving in the skies,
Dear hands and feet and laughter-lighted face
And silk that hinted at the body's grace.

But no-one seems to know quite what to say
    (Friends are so altered by the passing years):
'Well, anyhow, it's not so cold today' –
    And thus we try to dissipate our fears.
'*I am the Resurrection and the Life*':
Strong, deep and painful, doubt inserts the knife.

Executive

I am a young executive. No cuffs than mine are cleaner;
I have a Slimline brief-case and I use the firm's Cortina.
In every roadside hostelry from here to Burgess Hill
The *maîtres d'hôtel* all know me well and let me sign the bill.

You ask me what it is I do. Well actually, you know,
I'm partly a liaison man and partly P.R.O.
Essentially I integrate the current export drive
And basically I'm viable from ten o'clock till five.

For vital off-the-record work – that's talking transport-wise –
I've a scarlet Aston-Martin – and does she go? She flies!
Pedestrians and dogs and cats – we mark them down for
    slaughter.
I also own a speed-boat which has never touched the water.

She's built of fibre-glass, of course. I call her 'Mandy Jane'
After a bird I used to know – No soda, please, just plain –
And how did I acquire her? Well to tell you about that
And to put you in the picture I must wear my other hat.

I do some mild developing. The sort of place I need
Is a quiet country market town that's rather run to seed.
A luncheon and a drink or two. A little *savoir faire* –
I fix the Planning Officer, the Town Clerk and the Mayor.

And if some preservationist attempts to interfere
A 'dangerous structure' notice from the Borough Engineer
Will settle any buildings that are standing in our way –
The modern style, sir, with respect, has really come to stay.

Meditation on a Constable Picture

Go back in your mind to that Middlesex height
Whence Constable painted the breeze and the light
As down out of Hampstead descended the chaise
To the wide-spreading valley, half-hidden in haze:

The slums of St Giles's, St Mary'bone's farms,
And Chelsea's and Battersea's riverside charms,
The palace of Westminster, towers of the Abbey
And Mayfair so elegant, Soho so shabby,

The mansions where lilac hangs over brown brick,
The ceilings whose plaster is floral and thick,
The new stucco terraces facing the park,
The odorous alleyways, narrow and dark,

The hay barges sailing, the watermen rowing
On a Thames unembanked which was wide and slow-flowing,
The street-cries rebounding from pavements and walls
And, steeple-surrounded, the dome of St Paul's.

No market nor High Street nor square was the same
In that cluster of villages, London by name.
Ere slabs are too tall and we Cockneys too few,
Let us keep what is left of the London we knew.

Back from Australia

Cocooned in Time, at this inhuman height,
   The packaged food tastes neutrally of clay.
   We never seem to catch the running day
But travel on in everlasting night
With all the chic accoutrements of flight:
   Lotions and essences in neat array
   And yet another plastic cup and tray.
'Thank you *so* much. Oh no, I'm quite all right.'

At home in Cornwall hurrying autumn skies
   Leave Bray Hill barren, Stepper jutting bare,
     And hold the moon above the sea-wet sand.
The very last of late September dies
   In frosty silence and the hills declare
     How vast the sky is, looked at from the land.

Fruit

Now with the threat growing still greater within me,
   The Church dead that was hopelessly over-restored,
The fruit picked from these yellowing Worcestershire orchards
   What is left to me, Lord?

To wait until next year's bloom at the end of the garden
   Foams to the Malvern Hills, like an inland sea,
And to know that its fruit, dropping in autumn stillness,
   May have outlived me.

For Patrick, ætat: LXX*

How glad I am that I was bound apprentice
To Patrick's London of the 1920s.
Estranged from parents (as we all were then),
Let into Oxford and let out again,
Kind fortune led me, how I do not know,
To that Venetian flat-cum-studio
Where Patrick wrought his craft in Yeoman's Row.

For Patrick wrote and wrote. He wrote to live:
What cash he had left over he would give
To many friends, and friends of friends he knew,
So that the 'Yeo' to one great almshouse grew –
Not a teetotal almshouse, for I hear
The clink of glasses in my memory's ear,
The spurt of soda as the whisky rose
Bringing its heady scent to memory's nose
Along with smells one otherwise forgets:
Hairwash from Delhez, Turkish cigarettes,
The reek of Ronuk on a parquet floor
As parties came cascading through the door:
Elizabeth Ponsonby in leopard-skins
And Robert Byron and the Ruthven twins,
Ti Cholmondeley, Joan Eyres Monsell, Bridget Parsons,
And earls and baronets and squires and squarsons –
'Avis, it's *ages*! . . . Hamish, but it's *aeons* . . .'
(Once more that record, the Savoy Orpheans).

Leader in London's preservation lists
And least Wykehamical of Wykehamists:
Clan chief of Paddington's distinguished set,
Pray go on living to a hundred yet!

* Patrick Balfour, 3rd Baron Kinross, b. 1904.

1940

As I lay in the bath the air was filling with bells;
Over the steam of the window, out in the sun,
From the village below came hoarsely the patriot yells
And I knew that the next World War had at last begun.
As I lay in the bath I saw things clear in my head:
Ten to one they'd not bother to bomb us here,
Ten to one that they'd make for the barracks instead –
As I lay in the bath, I certainly saw things clear.
As I started to dry, came a humming of expectation;
Was it the enemy planes or was it young Jack
And the rest of the gang who have passed in their aviation
Setting across to Berlin to make an attack?
As the water gurgled away I put on a shirt,
I put on my trousers, and parted what's left of my hair;
And the humming above increased to a roaring spurt
And a shuddering thud drove all the bells from the air,
And a shuddering thud drove ev'rything else to silence.
There wasn't a sound, there wasn't a soul in the street,
There wasn't a wall to the house, there wasn't a staircase;
There was only the bathroom linoleum under my feet.
I called, as I always do, I called to Penelope,
I called to the strong with the petulant call of the weak;
There lay the head and the brown eyes dizzily open,
And the mouth apart but the tongue unable to speak;
There lay the nut-shaped head that I love for ever,
The thin little neck, the turned-up nose and the charms
Of pouting lips and lashes and circling eyebrows;
But where was the body? and where were the legs and arms?
And somewhere about I must seek in the broken building
Somewhere about they'll probably find my son.
Oh bountiful Gods of the air! Oh Science and Progress!
You great big wonderful world! Oh what have you done?

The Ballad of George R. Sims*

It's an easy game, this reviewin' – the editor sends yer a book,
Yer puts it down on yer table and yer gives it a 'asty look,
An' then, Sir, yer writes about it as though yer 'ad read it all
    through,

And if ye're a pal o' the author yer gives it a good review.

But if the author's a wrong 'un – and *some* are, as I've 'eard
    tell –
Or if 'e's a stranger to yer, why then yer can give him 'ell.
So what would yer 'ave me do, Sir, to humour an editor's
    whims,
When I'm pally with Calder-Marshall, and never knew
    George R. Sims?

It is easy for you to deride me and brush me off with a laugh
And say 'Well, the answer's potty – yer review it just 'arf and
    'arf' –
For I fear I must change my tune, Sir, and pump the bellows
    of praise
And say that both 'alves are good, Sir, in utterly different ways.

I'm forgettin' my cockney lingo – for I lapse in my style now
    and then
As Sims used to do in his ballads when he wrote of the Upper
    Ten –
'Round in the sensuous galop the high-born maids are swung
Clasped in the arms of *roués* whose vice is on every tongue'.

'It was Christmas Day in the workhouse' is his best known
    line of all,
And this is his usual metre, which comes, as you may recall,
Through Tennyson, Gordon, Kipling and on to the Sergeants'
    Mess,
A rhythm that's made to recite in, be it mufti or evening dress.

Now Arthur shows in his intro that George R. Sims was a
  bloke
Who didn't compose his ballads as a sort of caustic joke;
He cared about social justice but he didn't aim very high
Though he knew how to lay on the sobstuff and make his
  audience cry.

The village church on the back-drop is painted over for good,
The village concerts are done for where the Young Reciter
  stood,
The magic-lantern is broken and we laugh at the mission
  hymns –
We laugh and we well might weep with the Ballads of
  George R. Sims.

* This was a verse review in the *New Statesman* (October 25, 1968) of a
selection of George R. Sims' Ballads introduced by Arthur Calder-
Marshall.